Published in 2024 by Mortimer Children's
An imprint of Welbeck Children's Limited,
part of the Welbeck Publishing Group
Offices in: London - 20 Mortimer Street, London W1T 3JW
& Sydney - Level 17, 207 Kent St, Sydney NSW 2000 Australia
www.welbeckpublishing.com

Text, design, and layout © Welbeck Children's Limited 2024

ISBN 978 1 83935 276 8

Printed in Dubai

10 9 8 7 6 5 4 3 2 1

Please note that some of the foods mentioned in this book are allergens or may contain
allergens. Please check any ingredients carefully if you have a known food allergy to
avoid an allergic reaction.

BE MORE WEDNESDAY

HANNAH CATHER

MORTIMER

CONTENTS

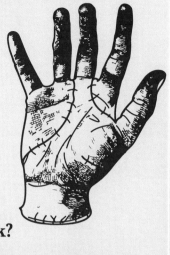

WELCOME

It's a dark world dripping with gore and goth-core, every day of the week. Wednesday is fierce and fearless, with an acid tongue and a razor-sharp wit. She's armed with killer comebacks and bulletproof putdowns, a sting in her tail, and a cold, cold heart. An outcast among outcasts...not that she cares.

Turn the page to find all you need to know about this goth icon—from character profiles, yucky recipes, and monochrome style tips, to gothic history, book recs, and creepy crafts, not to mention an inside look at her hobbies, school, and that infamous family. Learn how to inject some Weds into your life and it'll become darker in all the right ways.

It's time to embrace your dark side.

It's time to

BE MORE WEDNESDAY...

TO THE WORLD OF WEDNESDAY ADDAMS

WEDNESDAY ADDAMS

IT'S IN A NAME

Wednesday's name comes from the old nursery rhyme "Monday's Child"—you can read all about it on page 60. But did you know that her middle name is Friday, as she was born on Friday the 13th?

COLOR ALLERGY

Morticia says Weds has a "color allergy"—for her, it's monochrome or go home. In the 2022 TV series *Wednesday* (aired on Netflix), she even gets a custom black uniform at Nevermore Academy.

EXTRA DIGITS

Wednesday is said to have six toes on one foot, as her original creator, the US cartoonist Charles Addams, decided to give an extra digit to his character.

PSYCHIC ABILITIES

In the 2022 TV series, Wednesday has psychic powers, inherited from Morticia. She's known as a "raven," which means her visions are darker and more macabre. The powers need to be managed, though, or they can lead to madness.

HOBBIES

Can you count sarcasm as a hobby? No, it's a way of life. Otherwise, Wednesday loves to write and has author aspirations. She enjoys cello playing and fencing, too.

DETECTIVE ADDAMS

Not only is Wednesday a budding detective writer in the 2022 show (though unsuccessful, as her stories are deemed to be too morbid—go figure), but she becomes a real-life detective in a murky murder mystery.

In the **1991** *Addams Family* movie, Wednesday was played by Christina Ricci.

GET THE
Wednesday Addams LOOK

The Wednesday Addams look is iconic. Think dark academia/preppy mixed with Victoriana and emo edge, plus all-out goth core. But goth core doesn't have to mean goth bore...

PALETTE

Black, black, and more black, because color makes Wednesday "break out into hives." She does allow a few alternate shades—some white or gray won't kill anyone, after all—but that noir is necessary.

HAIR DO

One of THE most important elements of Wednesday's style is on her head. No, it's not a death stare, but her hair. Follow these rules:

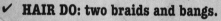

✔ HAIR DO: two braids and bangs.
✗ HAIR DON'T: anything else.

FIENDISH FOOTWEAR

Chunky shoes are a must for all that stomping around. The choices are a lace-up shoe (school vibes) or a bulky boot (a bit punk, a lot practical). A platform sneaker, too, if it's a comfy core kinda day.

TAILORING

Smart blazers, crisp lines and tailored pieces add perfectly to the dark academia aesthetic of Weds. She's serious, she's smart, she's classroom chic.

PATTERNS

Who said an all-dark attire isn't fun? Wednesday's wardrobe adds in stripes and checks for a pattern injection. Don't be fooled: it's all still strictly monochrome, but it's something.

THE DRESS-AND-COLLAR COMBO

The ultimate Wednesday Addams look, because nothing says Wednesday more than a black dress with a white Peter Pan or pilgrim collar. When this combo comes together, it's (black) magic.

Oh, one final accessory: forget to smile. There's no need for that face ache.

THE ADDAMS FAMILY TREE

UNCLE FESTER

Gomez's brother. Fester is one of the more mysterious family members; he can conduct electricity, and is a career criminal.

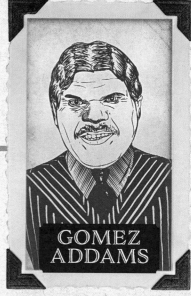

GOMEZ ADDAMS

The patriarch of the family, ex-student of Nevermore, and "the one who got all the brains" according to his brother, Fester.

WEDNESDAY ADDAMS

The older Addams child. Budding author and psychic, she is prone to an acerbic comeback, loves writing, and dislikes...most people.

"They're creepy and they're kooky, mysterious and spooky..." Find out who's who in the Addams family tree.

MORTICIA ADDAMS
(née Frump)

The matriarch of the family, who comes from a long line of witches. She met Gomez at Nevermore Academy.

OPHELIA FRUMP

Morticia's sister and her opposite in many ways—she's more positive and light, in both personality and clothing choice.

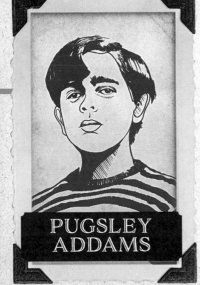

PUGSLEY ADDAMS

The younger Addams child, with a love-hate relationship with Wednesday. Yet to show psychic abilities, but who knows?

GOODY ADDAMS

In the 2022 series, she is an ancestor from the 1600s and one of the original outcasts. She has the same psychic powers as Wednesday, and they meet in Wednesday's visions.

WHICH ADDAMS FAMILY MEMBER ARE YOU?

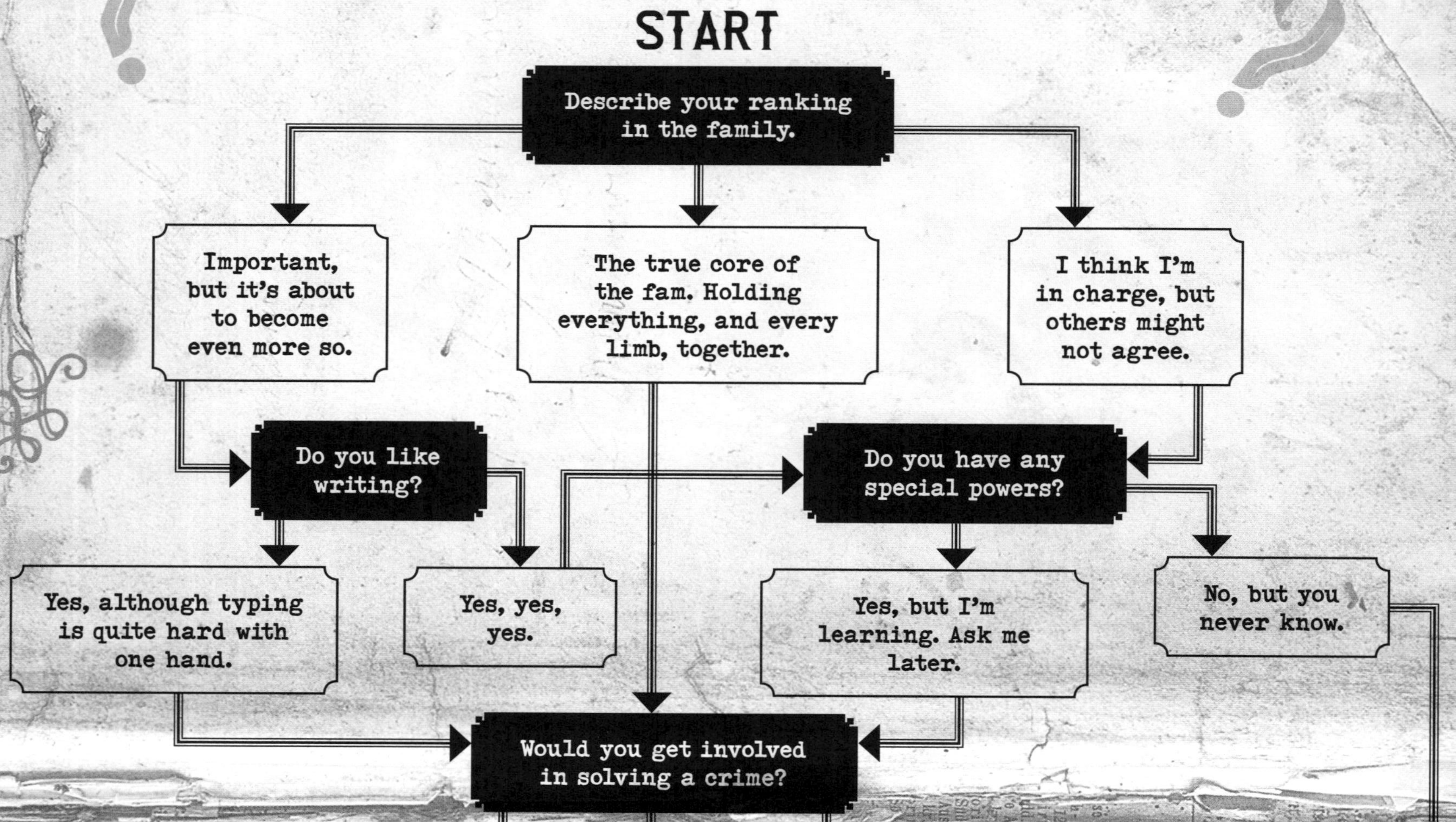

START

Describe your ranking in the family.

→ I think I'm in charge, but others might not agree.

→ The true core of the fam. Holding everything, and every limb, together.

→ Important, but it's about to become even more so.

Do you have any special powers?

→ No, but you never know.

→ Yes, but I'm learning. Ask me later.

Do you like writing?

→ Yes, yes, yes.

→ Yes, although typing is quite hard with one hand.

Would you get involved in solving a crime?

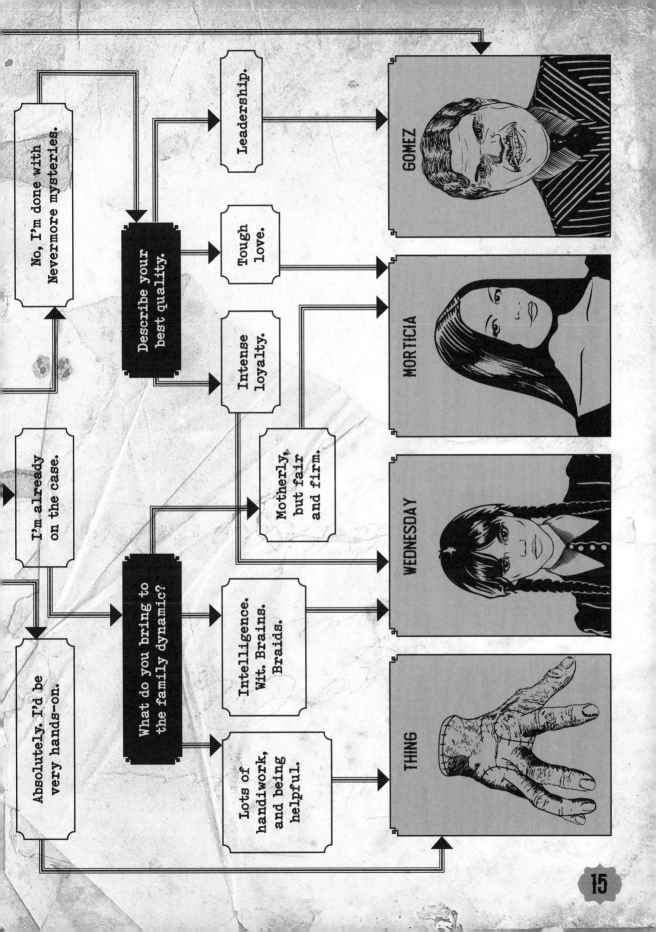

No, I'm done with Nevermore mysteries.

I'm already on the case.

Absolutely. I'd be very hands-on.

Describe your best quality.

Leadership.

Tough love.

Intense loyalty.

Motherly, but fair and firm.

What do you bring to the family dynamic?

Intelligence. Wit. Brains. Braids.

Lots of handiwork, and being helpful.

GOMEZ

MORTICIA

WEDNESDAY

THING

> I like being an **ISLAND.** A well-fortified one surrounded by **SHARKS.**

Wednesday Addams,
Wednesday **(2022 TV series)**

BEST MODERN GOTHIC BOOKS

Full of dreadful characters, deep secrets, black magic, and death, these are the kind of books that Wednesday would surely enjoy.

Gallant **by V. E. Schwab**
A mysterious letter brings Olivia Prior home, but no one is expecting her—not least the ghouls in the hallway...
You'll love this if: family spooky sagas are right up your street.

Anna Dressed in Blood **by Kendare Blake**
Cas is a teen with a strange career: he kills the dead. Anna was murdered in 1958 and she's seeking revenge...
You'll love this if: you love a relationship founded on death.

The Ravens **by Kass Morgan and Danielle Page**
The Ravens are sorority witches—their friendships are put to the test when a dark power invades their college.
You'll love this if: campus drama mixed with magic is your bag.

His Hideous Heart, **edited by Dahlia Adler**
Wednesday knows there's no one like Edgar Allan Poe. Here are 13 of his wicked stories, reimagined by current authors.
You'll love this if: you're a Poe fan, but love a fresh take.

Through the Woods **by Emily Carroll**
Five chilling stories about the horror that awaits you in the woods and the journeys into (and hopefully out of) them.
You'll love this if: you don't mind a surprise in the woods.

Turn to page 35 for classic gothic reads.

DINAL RED INK

NEVERMORE ACADEMY

Welcome to Nevermore! Founded in 1791 as "an academic institution that nurtures outcasts, freaks, and monsters," the school from the 2022 TV series *Wednesday* provides a place for extraordinary students to master their powers.

POE INSPIRED

Poe is the most famous alumnus of the academy and the school is said to be named after Poe's iconic raven (from the poem of the same name), whose persistent reply is "Nevermore."

ANNUAL EVENTS

Parent's Day/Weekend—when the students' parents visit for a weekend.
Outreach Day—the students visit the nearby town of Jericho to meet their normie neighbors.
Edgar Allan Poe Cup—a canoe race to Raven Island to grab flags and return them to the finish line, which has been running since 1897.
Rave'N—the annual Nevermore ball, for both normies and outcasts.

SCHOOL MOTTO

"UNITAS EST INVICTA"

OR

"UNITY IS INVINCIBLE"

CLUBS:

Séance Society—Morticia was once President of this group.

Pitch Slaps Club—a choir, comprising mainly sirens.

Archery—a place to sharpen your arrow-slinging skills. Perfect.

Nevermore Hummers—a beekeeping club, whose president is Eugene Ottinger.

UNIFORM ⇒ ➔

Students must wear a purple-and-black outfit, notably a striped blazer. However, if you're Wednesday and you have an intense allergy to color, it's monochrome. As a fellow student says, "You're in black and white. Like a living Instagram filter." Gorgons can wear beanie hats to cover their snake hair, and sirens wear a necklace that cancels out their siren voice.

THE PERFECT NIGHT (MARE)

Even outcasts need sleepovers. So why not lure an accomplice or two over for a night of style, scaring, and oversharing?

FOOD & DRINK

The trick here is to create some sumptuous yet spooky snacks, but you don't need to go too gimmicky—check out pages 22 for some ideas. Whatever you choose, a midnight feast is essential.

Turn to page 70 for devilish drink ideas.

ACTIVITIES
- Storytelling—who can tell the spookiest story?
- Gothic makeover—choose your most vanilla friend and goth them up for a change!
- Henna tattoos—ideal for wannabe witches.

WHAT TO WEAR

Encourage everyone to dress up –
black is a must, obviously.
But if someone isn't into it, and
just wants to tag along in their own
clothes, let them. We don't judge!

Check
out page 42 for
the ultimate
goth-casual
look.

WATCHLIST You can't go wrong with these darkly delicious movies.

- *A Monster Calls*
- *Something Wicked This Way Comes*
- *Wuthering Heights*
- *The Dark Crystal*

- *Cat People*
- *The Phantom of the Opera*
- *Monster House*
- *The Innocents*

For a seasonal
twist, how about
*The Nightmare
Before Christmas?*

KILLER SNACKS

A full stomach is important. Try one of these disgustingly good snacks next time you need a wicked treat, or save them for a spooky sleepover and the inevitable midnight munchies.

Making jelly is fun, but it's even better to add strange things into the concoction. Start by making up the jelly (following the pack's instructions) and then pour the mixture into little pots. Add gummies into each one, making sure that the sweets are suitably scary— like mouths, teeth, and bugs. Leave to set.

Blobby Jelly

This devilish desert never disappoints. And bonus: it's a real chocolatey treat, too. Break up some chocolate cookies, add in some crumbled chocolate muffin, and stir. Then melt some chocolate and add to the crumbly mixture. Separate into little pots and add in some gummy worms and bugs.

Dirt Cup

Graveyard Dip

For a perfectly awful party centerpiece, add your favourite dipping source to a bowl and stick in some tortillas like mini gravestones. For a bit more effort, add ghostly daubs of sour cream!

Dip strawberries into melted white chocolate and place on a tray. Put the tray into the freezer for 15 minutes. Once set, it's time to decorate. Add chocolate drops for eyes and mouths—or use blueberries for bulging eyes.

Spooky Strawbs

WHO'S WHO IN NEVERMORE

Siren

Gorgon

Meet the people/beings/things that reside inside the hallowed, haunted walls of the 2022 TV series' school. As Wednesday herself finds out, the school has "many flavors of outcast."

STUDENT GROUPS:

VAMPIRES—wear dark glasses so they can go out in the light, are allergic to garlic, and have lived for hundreds of years.

WEREWOLVES—human-like but with werewolf qualities, such as long claws and eating a largely red-meat diet. They are known to be loud and will "wolf out" in certain moons.

GORGONS—human-like apart from having snakes instead of hair. If someone looks directly at the snakes, they will turn into stone—which is why gorgons wear hats.

SIRENS—manipulative with powerful skills of persuasion. They have mermaid-like qualities and grow fins and tails when they come into contact with water.

PSYCHICS—their abilities include having visions of the future and the past, moving objects through mind power, warping reality, and bringing art to life.

TEACHERS:

Larissa Weems—Principal of the school, with shapeshifting powers. Morticia's roommate when they were both students.

Marilyn Thornhill—Botanical Sciences Teacher and Wednesday's "dorm mom." She is the only "normie" that the school has on its staff.

Coach Vlad—Fencing Coach.

ALUMNI:

EDGAR ALLAN POE

MORTICIA ADDAMS

GOMEZ ADDAMS

COUSIN ITT

LARISSA WEEMS

FUN FACT!

Marilyn Thornhill is played by Christina Ricci in the 2022 TV series. She also played the role of a younger Wednesday Addams in the two 1990s *Addams Family* films.

Larissa Weems

Marilyn Thornhill

WHICH NEVERMORE CLIQUE ARE YOU?

START

Do you like being in a clique?

- No, I prefer to see myself as an outcast among outcasts.
- Only if I'm in charge of the group.
- I love it. I work best as part of a pack.

Have you ever had a strange vision?

- More and more often.
- Never, but I wish I could see the future.

What's your favorite accessory for your uniform?

- I never go out without a hat.
- Dark glasses. For fashion, and to block all daylight.

How are your powers of persuasion?

I've got other powers to think about.

The absolute best. Unrivaled.

Good. If I'm in the mood.

Are you an animal lover?

How does a full moon affect you?

It gives me a howling good time.

Snakes are my thing— just check out my head.

Nothing is better than a funky, furry friend.

I always feel extra thirsty.

Makes me so happy I want to sing.

THE PSYCHICS

THE GORGONS

THE WEREWOLVES

THE VAMPIRES

THE SIRENS

WEDNESDAY PLAYLIST, PART 1

Find the full Wednesday playlist below, to pick at like a bone —split up by mood and genre. Why don't you sit back, press play, and let the music drag you right back to Nevermore...

Edith Piaf

UPBEAT

Blonde Redhead: "Sciuri Sciura"
Magdalena Bay: "The Beginning"
Hoku: "Perfect Day"—also a big song in *Legally Blonde*!
Rhythmking: "Can't Stop"
Henry Parsley and Amy Caddies
McKnight: "Levels"
Bravo and Immortal Girlfriend: "Someone Like You"
RAC (feat. Pink Feathers): "It's A Shame"
The Cramps: "Goo Goo Muck"—used for Wednesday's iconic dance scene
Dua Lipa: "Physical"

CHILLED

Beach House: "Space Song"—this one went viral on TikTok. Recognize it?
Roy Orbison: "In Dreams"
Wolf Larson: "If I Be Wrong"
Edith Piaf: "Non, Je Ne Regrette Rien" meaning "No, I regret nothing."
Chavela Vargas: "La Llorona"
Birthday Girls: "Secrets"
Carmita Jiménez: "Tierra Rica"

Turn to page 73 for more playlists.

One
need not be
a CHAMBER—
to be HAUNTED

**Emily Dickinson,
American poet
(1830–1886)**

THE WEDNESDAY ADDAMS DANCE

If you haven't seen the Wednesday Addams dance from the 2022 TV series, where have you been? Learn the moves below.

CLAW ARMS

Raise hands to elbow-height and turn your hands into claws. Move them from right to left, sweeping them from side to side.

FLAMENCO ARMS

Raise one arm so your hand is at head height and the opposite arm is chest height, but horizontal. Once in place, fluidly circle your wrists, curling your fingers around. Repeat on the other side, moving forward.

SIDE SHUFFLE

Make fists with your hands and join them at the knuckles, so your arms are chest-height and parallel to the floor. Start moving to one side by twisting your hips to that side, then straightening up. Repeat.

BODY FLING

Raise your arms up and fling your whole body down like a broken rag doll. Wednesday does this a number of times in the dance, with both arms together and then separately, too.

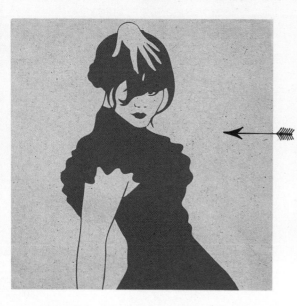

THE "THING" STEP—inspired by

Wednesday's handy friend, move your hands around your body as though they have a mind of their own. One hand could appear on the top of your head, or run from one shoulder to the next, or tap yourself on the shoulder.

THE ADDAMS FAMILY HISTORY

You might think you know about the Addams Family, but dive into its long and interesting background below to discover dark facts, black sheep and unusual beginnings.

CARTOON CREATION

The Addams Family started life as a series of one-panel cartoons in the New Yorker, by Charles Addams, the first of which hit the page in 1938. Addams would go on to illustrate nearly 60 cartoons of the Addams family.

GOTHIC INSPO

Addams was influenced by the spooky gothic buildings of his hometown, Westfield, New Jersey, which was full of sprawling Victorian mansions and creepy graveyards. The cartoon put the family's house on Cemetery Ridge, which is...apt.

Although the recent Addams Family animations have been CGI, they first appeared in cartoon form in 1973.

The Addams Family musical first opened in 2010 and contained hit songs like 'When You're An Addams'.

LOOMING LEGACY

The family has bred many offshoots including video games, multiple TV series, books, films—both animated and live-action—and a Tony-nominated Broadway musical.

DANCE MOVES

You might think that Wednesday is the dancer of the family, but her iconic moves weren't the first time a member of the Addams clan started a craze. Believe it or not, Lurch—the family's super-tall butler—created "The Lurch" dance, complete with a novelty single of the same name. It was huge in the 60s—ask your grandma!

Lurch in the 2022 TV series

> ## I know always that I am an **OUTSIDER**, a **STRANGER...**

From "The Outsider" by American horror writer H. P. Lovecraft (1890-1937)

BEST CLASSIC GOTHIC BOOKS

Wednesday's love of Poe and Mary Shelley is crystal clear, but here are some other classic gothic horror books to feast on.

Carmilla by Joseph Sheridan

An early work of vampire fiction (pre-Dracula!) about a young woman who is preyed upon by a female vampire named Carmilla. A book of die-hard obsessions and beastly nightmares.

The Strange Case of Dr. Jekyll and Mr. Hyde by Robert Louis Stevenson

A powerful novella on the duality of human nature. On one side Dr. Jekyll is a kind, intelligent scientist; on the other is Mr. Hyde, his evil alter ego. It doesn't end well.

Dracula by Bram Stoker

The infamous horror story about the terrifying happenings in Count Dracula's castle in Transylvania, and then in Whitby and London, and his poor victims. Every last drop of them.

The Picture of Dorian Gray by Oscar Wilde

A man stays looking young, while his portrait in the attic ages. A story about the obsession with beauty and youth, and how selling your soul for them will only ever end dreadfully.

We Have Always Lived in the Castle by Shirley Jackson

A dark family mystery about the isolated lives of Merricat, Constance, and Uncle Julian, who live as outcasts after a family tragedy. When their isolation is interrupted by their cousin Charles, all hell breaks loose.

DRESS TO KILL

The black frothy dream of a dress that Wednesday wears in her dance scene in the 2022 TV series is a moment. Just the right amount of party vibe, with just the right amount of don't-care-about-the-party vibe—the perfect contradiction.

Now it's your turn to create an outfit from your wildest imaginings. It could be for a prom or an adventure; it could be practical or not; it could be black or...black (other colors are available). Sketch it out on the right and see what you can come up with.

Did you know?

The costume team of the 2022 TV show had to make copies of the party dress worn by Jenna Ortega, as the dance scene involves a downpour of blood—covering everyone and everything!

IDEAS

Sketch your ideas here:

GOTH HISTORY

The goth scene and look is ingrained into today's culture, but how did it all start? Check out its backgrounds, beginnings, and influences below.

BACKGROUND

The goth subculture started life in the UK in the early 1980s—it was music-influenced, not fashion-influenced, as is sometimes believed. Post-punk paved the way, and gave way, to goth rock.

FASHION

Goth fashion's influences include punk, Victoriana, and the New Romantics. The look often includes fishnets, studs, leather, platform boots, band t-shirts, velvet and lace, and endless black. Don't be a "goth-in-a-box" or a "mall goth", though; make sure to customize and thrift your cold little heart out. Black nail varnish and black eye makeup are essential.

FUN FACT!

A 'Baby Bat' is the term used by older goths toward any newbie to the goth life, who is unfamiliar with the subculture, but trying to get a feel for it.

Siouxsie Sioux, goth pioneer

Sisters of Mercy

MUSIC ORIGINS

'Bela Lugosi's Dead,' a single by English post-punk band Bauhaus, is often seen as the first gothic rock record. It was recorded in one take during a six-hour session and was the first song the band recorded together. Its gothic lyrics, full of bats, funerals, and virgin brides, set the tone for gothic music and contemporary goth culture.

Other goth bands include Siouxsie and the Banshees, Echo and the Bunnymen, London After Midnight, She Past Away, The Sisters of Mercy, The Cure, Joy Division, and Velvet Underground.

LEGACY

The goth scene is one of the most enduring subcultures—it doesn't seem to want to die, which is fitting. And not only does it survive, but it thrives, influencing many aspects of life including literature, philosophy, films, music, fashion, makeup, and art. Its darkness is everywhere.

HOW TO BE MORE WEDNESDAY

Wednesday's roomie in the 2022 TV series, Enid, finds herself asking "WWWD?"—"What Would Wednesday Do?" It's worth asking yourself the same question. There's a lot we can learn from our favorite goth gal. Here's how to be more Weds.

1
Simple, wear black.
They say black never goes out of fashion, which makes Weds an evergreen style queen. Or should that be everblack?

2
Do what you want.
Every day is all about you, and don't let anyone stand in your way.

3
Be loyal to your inner circle.
Wednesday's loyalty to her family and very close friends is undying—and this from a girl who loves death. Don't waste effort on spreading loyalty around. Keep a tight circle.

WWWD

4 Don't care what other people think, or go one step further and don't even think about what other people think. As Enid says of Weds, "Most people spend their entire lives pretending to give zero effs and you literally never had an eff to give."

5 Honesty is the best policy, even if the truth hurts. Some of Wednesday's truth bombs are painful, but say what you mean and say it straight, and people will respect it.

GOTH TIE-DYE

Tie-dye is the style that never dies, so why not give this to-die-for craft a try? Simply follow the steps and you'll be a die-hard tie-dyer in no time at all.

WHAT YOU'LL NEED
- White or pale t-shirt
- Clothing dyes (preferably black)
- Rubber bands
- Gloves and apron to wear
- Trash bags
- Plastic bag

1. Wash your t-shirt in the washing machine to get rid of any oil or dirt. This will help the dye attach to the material.

2. Set up a work area, preferably outside, with stuck-down large trash bags.

3. Fold and tie your garment. This can be done in lots of ways, but the easiest is simply to scrunch the garment up and wrap several rubber bands around the bundle.

The way you tie your dyed t-shirt influences the patterns you'll get.

Rinse the t-shirt well, or it will make all your clothes black in the wash. Wait, is that a plus?

4. Apply the dye by squirting it onto the tied-up garment. If you don't have squeezy bottles, this can also be painted on.

5. Let it rest! Put the garment in a plastic bag and leave in a sunny spot to dry for around 6 to 8 hours. Take a rest yourself, too.

6. Rinse with the rubber bands in place and under lukewarm water (until the water runs clear), then pop it in the washing machine.

7. Try again with socks, sweatshirts, hoodies, tote bags. You'll be dyeing-obsessed, if you weren't already.

Experiment with different patterns for shocking results.

JENNA ORTEGA

Who is the actor behind the braids?
Get to know more about Jenna Ortega, who plays
Wednesday in the 2022 TV series, below.

ON THE LACK OF BLINKING:

"At some point during the first couple of weeks of shooting, I did a take where I did not blink at all. And [director] Tim Burton said, "I don't want you to blink anymore.""

ON FIRST SEEING THE ADDAMS FAMILY:

"I was about 8 or 9, and I remember just being absolutely enamored. I always liked weird little things and I liked that they weren't the conventional family. And Wednesday, I wanted to be her so badly."

ON HER AUDITION WITH TIM BURTON:

"When I met [him] for my audition, I had stage blood and glycerin sweat and a massive cut on my face, and had been up for over 24 hours. I got on zoom and he actually laughed. It made me laugh."

ON BEING THE CHOREOGRAPHER OF THE "WEDS" DANCE:

"I'm not a dancer. I don't do any of that. I didn't sleep for two days. I found archival footage of goth kids dancing in clubs in the 80s. And then on the day, I thought 'let's see what happens.'"

FAST-TRACK FACTS

- Jenna voiced Disney's first Latina princess: Isabel in Elena of Avalor.
- She was first discovered when her mother posted a Facebook video of her.
- She was a vegan until she went to Romania to film Wednesday, where she became a pescatarian.
- She published her first book in 2021, called *It's All Love*.

FEELINGS, WHAT FEELINGS?

Wednesday might hide it, and hide it well, but part of what makes her reachable is that at the core of her darkness, there are feelings...even a little bit of goodness.

After all, Wednesday (reluctantly) makes friends, is fiercely loyal of her family, and experiences budding relationships. She may have a sour face throughout, but she's got some warm blood in her veins.

Weds might roll her eyes at these questions, but let's see how you're feeling: How are you really today?

What makes you happy?

What makes you miserable? (And not in a good way?)

The most interesting PLANTS grow in the SHADE.

Marilyn Thornhill,
Wednesday **(2022 TV series)**

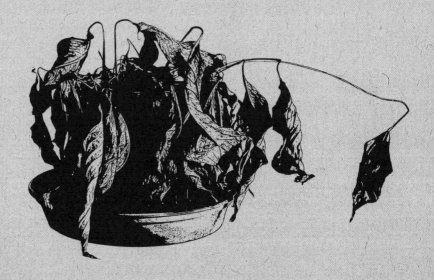

TOP TEEN-GOTH FILMS, PART 1

Corpse Bride

The Witches (2020)

Not all classics are old. Here are some more modern macabre movies...

If you like Tim Burton:
Edward Scissorhands
Sleepy Hollow

If you like light-hearted witchy vibes:
The Witches (the 1990 version, or the 2020 movie if you must)
Hocus Pocus

For some goth icon inspo:
Beetlejuice
The Craft

If you like animated films:
Corpse Bride
Coraline

For horror with an author protagonist:
Mary Shelley
Crimson Peak

PSYCHIC ABILITIES

Wednesday's psychic powers in the 2022 TV series are a blessing and a curse. Through them, she can see the future and the past, solve mysteries, connect with ancestors and anticipate dreadful happenings.

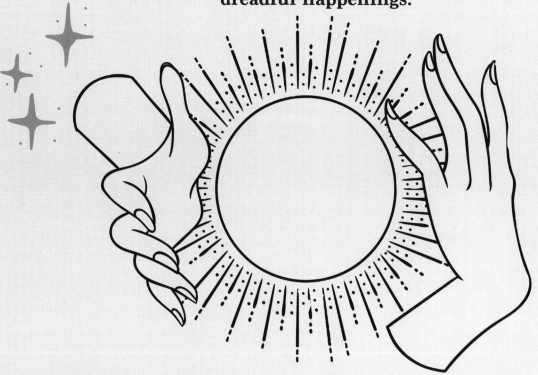

HOW THEY FEEL: When she has a vision, Weds tends to be standing upright, with eyes wide open and her head to the ceiling. As the visions get stronger, Weds is able to immerse herself and interact with them.

SOMETHING NEW: The powers are fairly new to Weds. So when she enters Nevermore, she is still getting used to the ever-strengthening abilities. Touch seems to set them off, whether that's touching a person or an object—they cannot be summoned on demand.

DOWN THE LINE: the psychic gift is generational and handed down from Morticia. But whereas Morticia is described as having "dove" abilities (a softer power, which tends to lean on more positive visions), Wednesday has "raven" abilities (stronger, darker, more powerful visions). Morticia warns that the ability needs to be controlled or it could send the psychic mad.

GOODY, GOODY: in one of her visions, Weds is able to interact with her ancestor (and doppelganger), Goody Addams. Weds asks for help in controlling her powers, to which Goody replies: "There is no controlling a raging river. You must learn to navigate it without drowning."

GOTH CORE CLAWS

Nails are useful for scratching, scraping, picking, and itching, but they can look good in the process. How about trying one of these goth-inspired designs on your claws?

Choose a light colour for the base, like white or gray, and build this up with a second layer. When that's dry, time for the fun part—the blood. Grab a red polish and a thin brush, and paint drips of red coming down from the top of the nail.

Bloody tips

Do a couple of layers of a light-coloured base. Using a small brush and black polish, draw diagonal lines from the bottom side of your nail to the top opposite side. Then draw webs in between these lines until complete.

Spiderwebs

Eyes in the dark

The definition of simple but effective, this spooky design starts by slapping* some black polish onto your nails Once dry, paint two white circles side by side anywhere on each nail, then do two smaller black dots inside these.

*Okay, painting neatly. (Or as neatly as you can be bothered to do.)

Witches love a vivid stripy stocking, and your nails will too. Think either orange, green, or purple in garish hues with parallel or crossing black stripes. Use a thin paintbrush and don't worry about the lines not looking perfect.

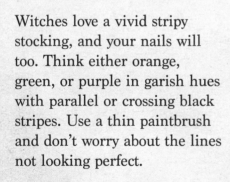

Witchy stripes

DETECTIVE NOTEPAD

Sometime you don't need a "Dear diary..." kind of vibe,
but a space to document important information
and observations.

Keep a beady, unblinking eye on everything around you and
note down anything untoward—you never know, you may need to
refer to it in a later investigation. Log the evidence below.
You could do this freehand or as a bullet journal,
with short, snappy, explosive little points.
Explosive is good...

Is someone acting strangely?

What was that noise in the dead of night?

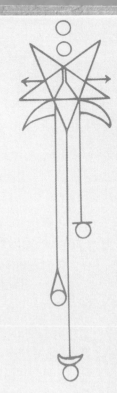

Did you overhear an odd conversation?

THING

FULL NAME

If you want to full-name him, he's "Thing T Thing," with the "T" standing for "Thing." The name is to show the mystery behind his character—that no one really knows who he is, where he comes from, or if he was ever part of a whole body.

NOT ALONE

He's not the only "Thing" out there. In previous series, there is mention of "Lady Fingers" and "Esmerelda," both female hands who also act as "handservants," as well as Thing's own parents. So keep an eye out for any stray decapitated hands...

HAND DAMAGE

The 2022 TV version of Thing is the first to have scars and stitches on the hand—to show the checkered past he's had. Or is it to show that he's been stitched together Frankenstein-style from multiple hands?

SEVERED HEAD

The Addams family's cartoonist creator, Charles Addams, originally had Thing as a decapitated head that would roll around the family house on ramps and pulleys. It was later decided that a severed hand might be a better option.

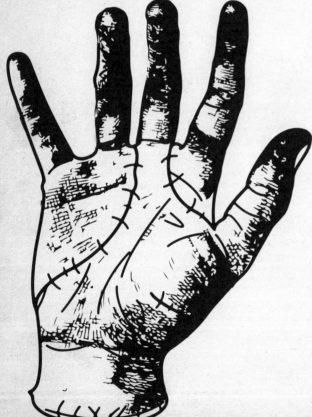

FUN FACT!

In the 2022 TV series, the actor who supplied a hand for Thing was a magician, Victor Dorobantu – not a professional actor.

RIGHT OR LEFT?

Do you think Thing is right-handed or left-handed? Think about it. He's actually a right-handed creature!

WHAT'S YOUR WEDNESDAY LOOK?

START

How long do you take to get ready?

No time at all. That's too much effort.

A while. I enjoy the process.

What's your take on an all-black look?

Do you care about what you're wearing?

I'll add a bit of color here and there. Not too much, just a bit.

It's perfect. Black never goes out of fash.

Yes, always. It's super-important.

Ugh. I dress up when I need to.

What is your fashion motto?

- Don't have one; don't want one.
- Dress for you. Not anyone else.
- Stay classic. Always.

Do you like making fashion statements?

- No thanks.
- If I'm in the mood.

Would you dress up for a party?

- Yes, but only in black.
- No, I'm never changing my look.

DRESS-DOWN WEDS
Stripy top. Jeans. Stompy boots or sneakers.

FANCY WEDNESDAY
Disco dress and an up-do.

THE CLASSIC WEDS LOOK
Black dress. White collar. Sorted.

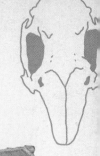

WEIRD WEEK

**Wednesday gets her name from
the poem below.**

Monday's child is fair of face

Tuesday's child is full of grace

Wednesday's child is full of woe

Thursday's child has far to go

Friday's child is loving and giving

Saturday's child works hard for a living

And the child that is born on the Sabbath Day

Is fair and wise and good in every way.

"Full of woe"? Very apt for Weds. This poem is basically a creepy old fortune-telling nursery rhyme, where you're meant to be able to tell what a child's personality will be based on the day of the week they were born.

Which day of the week were you born on? Does the description for that day sound like you, too?

_____

_____

_____

_____

_____

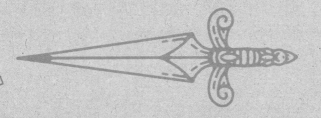

BEWARE

for I am

FEARLESS

and therefore

POWERFUL...

**From *Frankenstein*,
by English writer Mary Shelley
(1797-1851)**

HAUNTING READS

There aren't many things that Wednesday would claim to like, but writing is one of them. Check out some of her gothic writing icons below.

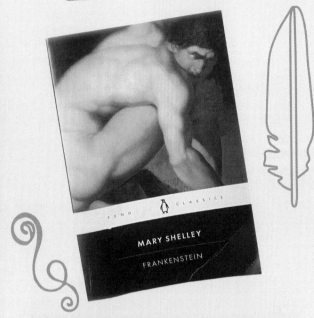

MARY SHELLEY
FRANKENSTEIN

MARY SHELLEY

The *Frankenstein* author is mentioned in the 2022 TV series, when Wednesday calls Shelley her "literary hero and nemesis."

EMILY BRONTË

With writing full of windswept moors, ghostly knocks on rain-splattered windows, utter heartbreak, untimely death, and generations of misery, Brontë provides plenty to inspire a woe-hungry Wednesday.

EDGAR ALLAN POE

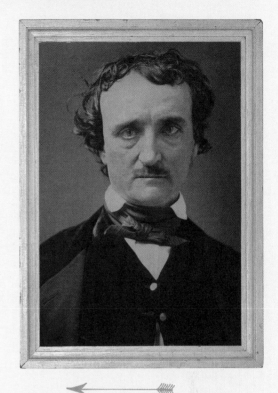

The eminent horror writer is referenced numerous times in the 2022 TV series, from the Poe cup (the Nevermore sports festival) to the Poe statue, as well as the labeling of Wednesday's psychic powers as "Raven," a nod to Poe's famous poem.

EMILY DICKINSON

Having written hundreds of poems on death, including "I Felt a Funeral, in my Brain," Emily Dickinson was no stranger to the macabre. She was also something of an eccentric in her lifetime, often wearing only white and living an isolated life.

Wednesday does her writing on a black typewriter—would you expect anything less?

FUN FACT!

in Edgar Allan Poe's poem "The Raven", an unnamed narrator descends into madness—in this decline, he comes across a raven. During their conversation about the narrator's lost love, the raven repeatedly uses a word in his replies, which is (drum roll) "Nevermore"—the name of Wednesday's school.

GARDEN GRAVESTONES

Gravestone decorations in your yard aren't just for Halloween, they're for life. Spend some time doing the creepy craft below and you'll be scaring the neighbors in no time.

WHAT YOU'LL NEED

- Cardboard
- Scissors
- Pens
- Lollipop sticks/twigs/gardening spikes.

1. Trace gravestone shapes onto cardboard —they could be tall and pointy, or in the shape of an angel, or boxy.
2. Cut them out, taking your time.
3. Color them in gray or black, using paint or pens.
4. Now decorate! Add your ghoulish words and drawings on one side of the gravestone.
5. Using regular tape/masking tape, attach a stick onto the back of each gravestone, leaving enough length at the bottom to stick in the ground.
6. All done! Put them outside and get ready for an outcry.

Ideas for gravestone messages...

RIP

REST IN PIECES

DIED ON SATURDAY BURIED BY WEDNESDAY

LET ME
OUT OF
HERE!

I'LL BE
BACK!

FUTURE
CORPSE
BRIDE

GOTH GIRL ICONS

Wednesday joins a host of ghoulish goth girl icons whose self-confidence and spiky attitudes inspire. They tend to have striking looks, a fondness for black, and an unmatched ability to deliver a deadpan retort.

JANIS IAN

The goth sidekick in the movie *Mean Girls*, Janis describes herself as "one of the greatest people you'll meet." She has an acidic tongue and is a fiercely loyal friend. Her clipped-up black hair and smudged eye makeup are a statement.

MARCELINE THE VAMPIRE QUEEN

A fun-loving vampire queen from the cartoon TV series Adventure Time. She likes the horror movie *Psycho* and plays an electric bass.

NANCY DOWNS

From the classic teen witch drama *The Craft*, Nancy is a goth witch who goes out of control with her powers. Her studded chocker, PVC trench coat, and precise makeup are a masterclass in the classic goth look. Take note.

Lydia Deetz

LYDIA DEETZ
From the 1988 movie *Beetlejuice*, Lydia is a witty, courageous teen goth with a penchant for an incredible hairdo, like Wednesday—you'll never unsee that spiky razor-sharp fringe and unruly half-up do.

LUCY LOUD
A deadpan, gloomy goth girl, with dark bangs and no trace of a smile —remind you of anyone? Lucy comes from the cartoon TV series *The Loud House*, in which a boy named Lincoln lives alongside his ten sisters.

WRITING PROMPTS

Call it a hobby, call it an obsession,
but Weds loves writing...and so can you.

Below are some mortifying prompts to lead
you into tales of woe and despair. These
prompts are the bones of the story and it's up
to you to flesh them out with gore and guts,
odd characters, and creepy dialogue.

She couldn't remember what she had done, but she had
a weapon in one hand and blood all over the other...

Once upon a time...wait, scrap that. This isn't a fairy tale.
This is a nightmare. And it begins with an ear-piercing
scream...

It took a moment to realize it, but it seemed she was in the very worst place she could possibly be in…

If she moved, they would hear her. She had to stay very still. She held her breath, but then…

HOW ABOUT: lighting some candles and reading your stories out loud to friends / family for a spooky storytelling sesh?

DISGUSTINGLY GOOD DRINKS

Don't forget to hydrate in between delivering spice and no-things nice to everyone. Try one of these dreadful drinks and you'll feel back on your ghoulish game before the last drop.

Squeeze **3 blood oranges** into a jar, add **1 tablespoon honey** and ½ **tablespoon vanilla extract**. Place the lid on the jar and shake it, baby. Add some **lime or lemon sparkling water** to this concoction, pop in some ice, and consume.

Blood-orange Mocktail

The perfect party drink: mix **orange soda (4 ¼ cups)**, **pineapple juice (1 ¾ cups)**, and **ginger ale (3 ¼ cups)** in a large bowl. Prep your glasses with a scoop of **vanilla ice cream** and pour the mixture over them. Easy!

Witches' Brew

Shock Hot Choc

Keep it simple with instant hot chocolate (with hot water or milk), then have fun with the decoration. How about **canned whipped cream covered in black, orange, and green sprinkles**, or tons of **chocolate drops and chocolate bugs** for a muddy take? Or draw some ghost faces (with an **edible marker**) onto **marshmallows**? Throw it all on top.

Take **5oz strawberries, 2 tablespoons lemon juice, ¼ cup water, 2 tablespoons sugar,** and **7oz crushed ice.** Pop all of the above into a blender and mix till you're happy with the consistency. If you're feeling extra sour, add some more lemon.

Sweet and Sour Slushies

"

There's a
FUN, FLIPPANT
side to me of course.
But I would much
rather be known as
the **ICE QUEEN**.

Siouxsie Sioux,
The Guardian 2005

"

WEDNESDAY PLAYLIST, PART 2

More magnificently moody music for you to sink your teeth into.

CLASSICAL

Vivaldi: "Four Seasons (Winter)"—played in the 2022 TV series *Wednesday* as an explosion erupts in Jericho's town square. Drama!
Umberto Giordano: "La Mamma Morta"
Saint-Saëns: "Danse Macabre"
Grieg: "In the Hall of the Mountain King"
Orff: "O Fortuna"

COVERS

Dominik Luke Johnson: "Gnossienne No 1" (originally by Erik Satie)
Apocalyptica: "Nothing Else Matters" (originally by Metallica)
Nevermore's acappella group "Don't Worry Be Happy" (originally by Bobby McFerrin)
Wednesday Addams, on top of the Nevermore Academy, no less): "Paint It Black" (originally by The Rolling Stones)

Metallica

COMEBACKS & QUIPS

Ever needed a biting comeback or an acidic one-liner? Memorize these woefully witty Wednesday-style barbs, and shoot them off just when you need them.

"Why do I wear black? So I'm ready for your funeral."

"My bark is worse than my bite. Actually, they're both bad."

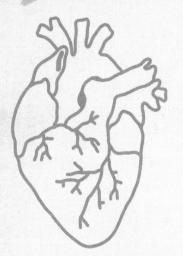

"I've got a voodoo doll with your name on it."

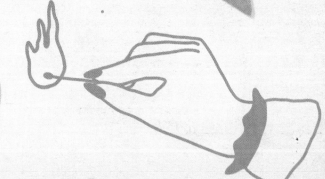

"You're giving me zombie vibes. Like death warmed up."

"If you listen reaaaallly closely... you can hear me not caring. At all."

"I'd suck the life out of you, but let's face it: you have no life."

GOMEZ AND MORTICIA

TWISTED HISTORY

According to the 2022 TV series, Wednesday's parents met while they were both students at Nevermore and fell madly in love. However, their initial bliss was tied up with a twisted love triangle involving another student, whose obsession with Morticia led to stalking, fighting, and murder. Gulp.

COUPLE STYLE

Gomez can always be found wearing a suit (pin-striped and sharp), while Morticia prefers a black, figure-hugging, floor-length dress. Their goth styles are perfect complements to each other.

PSYCHIC POWERS

While Gomez's powers are unconfirmed, Morticia has psychic abilities that began when she was a student at Nevermore. However, unlike Wednesday's "raven" psychic abilities, Morticia is known as a "dove" psychic, as her powers are less negative and strong.

WHICH NAME?

The creator of the Addams Family, American cartoonist Charles Addams, couldn't decide whether to call the patriarch Gomez or Repelli (a take on the word "repellent"). Actor John Astin, who played this character in the 1960s series, chose the former.

MAKEUP MISCHIEF AND MAYHEM

Make-up might not be the first thing on Wednesday's mind, but it's certainly not the last—as her smudgy eyes and painted lips show.

The goth spectrum is large, so go soft, go hard, or go home on the looks below—sketch, annotate, color, get creative. See it as a practice for doing the looks on yourself!

For colors, it's smoky blacks and browns, as well as nudes and—if color must be considered—deep plums and purples. It's all quite soft-goth—not too scary; there's no need as Wed's demeanour is more than terrifying enough. However, a harder goth look could include heavy eyeliner, dark statement lips, deliberately pasty complexion, and thick eyebrows.

THE SARCASM OF WEDNESDAY

Wednesday can throw shade like no one else. Each of her lines and quips pack a huge punch in the gut and drip with sarcasm.

When another student saves her in *Wednesday* Episode 1: "So you were guided by latent chivalry, the tool of the patriarchy, to extract my undying gratitude?"

Write some of your own wicked one-liners on the page opposite, or make a note of your favorite Wednesday ones.

GLOW JARS

Dim lighting is always preferable—this craft means you can set the scene at home, perfect for a spooky reading session or while writing horror stories. Just a normal night, then!

WHAT YOU'LL NEED

- jam jar
- paper
- pens
- tape
- battery-operated night light

1. Draw out a spooky design onto the middle of your paper. Some ideas are below.

2. When you're happy with your design, color it in and decorate.

3. Wrap the paper around the jar and stick together at the back.

4. Switch on the night light and place in the jar. Looking good!

5. Make a lot more, to really set the mood. And by mood, we mean "cozy downtime in a dingy dungeon."

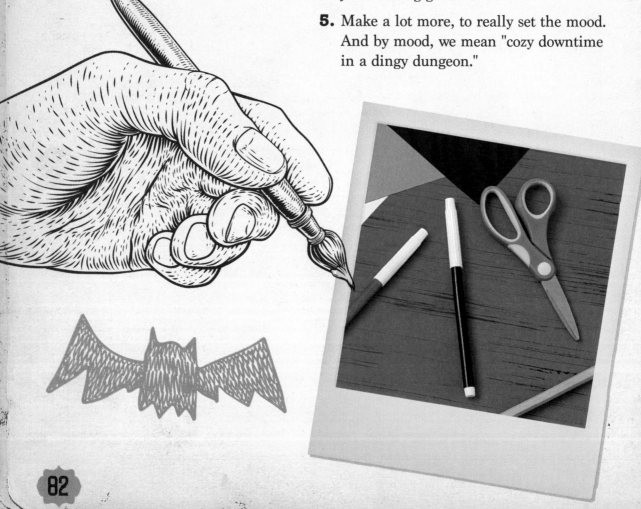

IDEAS

- Spooky Halloween pumpkin-style faces
- Spiders and spiderwebs
- Bats and bugs

Never to **SUFFER** would have been never to have been **BLESSED.**

**From "Mesmeric Revelation"
by American writer
Edgar Allan Poe
(1809-1849)**

TOP TEEN-GOTH FILMS, PART 2

Twilight

Warm Bodies

If you're still in the mood for more pitch-black movie masterpieces, try these out.

If you like super-surreal musicals:
Little Shop of Horrors
The Rocky Horror Picture Show

If vampires are your vibe:
The Lost Boys
Twilight (and its sequels *New Moon, Eclipse,* and *Breaking Dawn Parts I and II*)

For a mix of teen-angst and mystery:
Fright Night
Donnie Darko

Animation, but make it spooky...
The Nightmare Before Christmas
ParaNorman

If you like zombies and a giggle:
Warm Bodies
The Dead Don't Die

WHAT BREED OF GOTH ARE YOU?

START

If you had to choose a historical period to travel to, which would it be?

Victorian. Love the mourning dress look.

New Romantic. But make it dark and distressed.

Any period that would teach me what I need to know about the goth scene.

What is your go-to dress-up look?

Frothy dark dress with neon touches.

Black top. Black fishnets. Black boots. Black eyeliner.

Name your favorite decade.

The late 70s. The beginnings of goth rock. So cool.

Now, I guess. But I'm very obsessed with the 80s too.

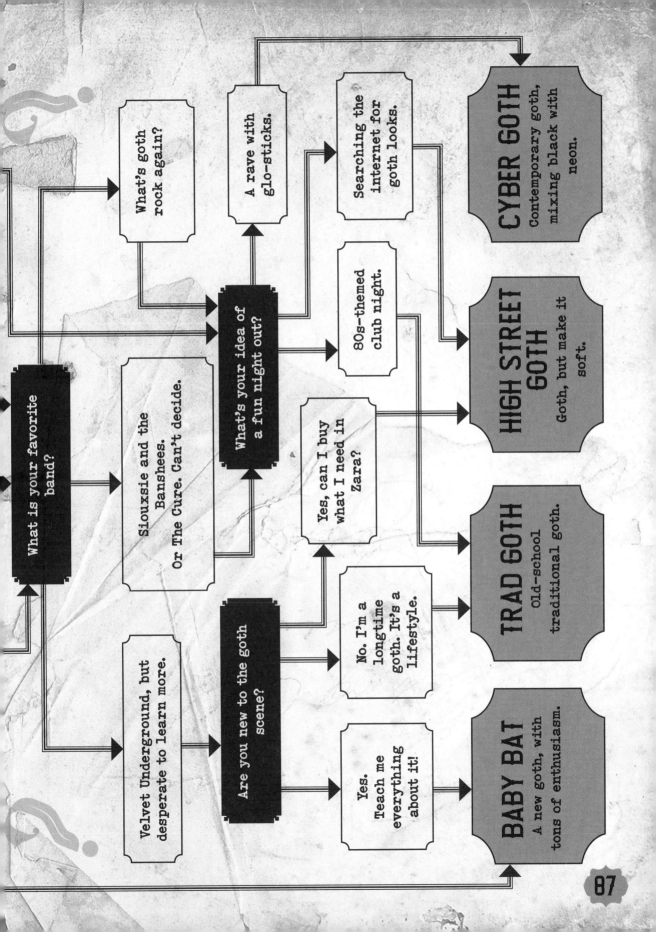

What is your favorite band?

- What's goth rock again?
- Siouxsie and the Banshees. Or The Cure. Can't decide.
- Velvet Underground, but desperate to learn more.

What's your idea of a fun night out?

- A rave with glo-sticks.
- Searching the internet for goth looks.
- 80s-themed club night.
- Yes, can I buy what I need in Zara?

Are you new to the goth scene?

- No. I'm a longtime goth. It's a lifestyle.
- Yes. Teach me everything about it!

CYBER GOTH
Contemporary goth, mixing black with neon.

HIGH STREET GOTH
Goth, but make it soft.

TRAD GOTH
Old-school traditional goth.

BABY BAT
A new goth, with tons of enthusiasm.

NO-SCREEN TIME

"I find social media to be a soul-sucking void of meaningless affirmation." Wednesday doesn't hold back. But she has a point—social media can be pretty antisocial. Here are some ideas for things you can do away from the screen:

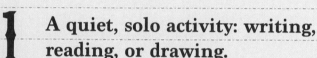

1 A quiet, solo activity: writing, reading, or drawing.

2 Start learning a musical instrument. Weds likes the cello; what would you pick up?

3 Be an amateur sleuth—keep an eye out for any strange goings-on.

4 Learn a dance. And there's nowhere better to start than the Wednesday Addams dance on page 30.

5 Bake something devilishly delicious. And don't share it. See page 22.

6 Spend time with people you actually like (if there are any).

ACTIVITY	HOW MUCH I HATED IT (on a scale of 1-10)	THE LEAST AWFUL THING ABOUT IT WAS

WEDNESDAY HAIR TUTORIAL

Wednesday is known for her hair, whether she means to be a style icon or not. See below for four different braid looks, in honor of the queen of braids herself.

The iconic twin braids

Wednesday without braids is just wrong. It doesn't work. And it's a simple style to do yourself: divide your hair down the middle, do a low braid on one side (starting from ear level), and tie at the end, then repeat on the other side. Ruffle up your bangs if you have them.

The up-do crown braids

Grab one braid, take it over your head (where a headband would sit), and pin it in place, then repeat with the other side. Tidy up any straggles with pins and hairspray, then spray the whole thing.

Create a simple side braid by collecting all hair to one side and braiding from ear level downward. If you're able to, make this into a French side braid.

Side braid

A bit of a curveball, but an eye-catching one. Put your hair into two high, braided pigtails. Grab each braid and twirl it around into a bun, fastening with pins.

DID YOU KNOW?

According to Tara McDonald, the 2022 TV series' hair and makeup designer, Wednesday's crown-braid up-do in the dance scene was inspired by Alexa Chung.

Space braids

" No existence is more **CONTEMPTIBLE** than that which is embittered by **FEAR**. "

From *The Mysteries of Udolpho* by English writer Ann Radcliffe (1764-1823)

TRICK OR... TRICK

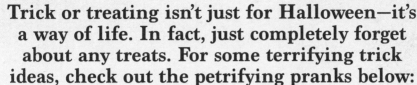

Trick or treating isn't just for Halloween—it's a way of life. In fact, just completely forget about any treats. For some terrifying trick ideas, check out the petrifying pranks below:

- Place cling film under the toilet seat and put the seat back down. The next visitor will get quite a surprise.

- Change all the clocks in your house to confuse everyone else.

- Write a creepy message, using a cotton bud and washing-up liquid, to the bathroom mirror, and it'll appear next time someone takes a shower. Try "I know what you did" or "I'm watching you!".

- Add a few drops of tomato ketchup to your hands and fake an injury. Screaming is optional.

- Hide between the curtains, or under the cushions on the sofa, and make someone jump when they enter the room.

- Add gummy bugs or eyeballs to ice cube trays with water. When frozen, add them to your victim's drink.

- Plaster pretend spiders and cockroaches all around the bathroom. Then complain about standards of cleanliness in this place...

SPOOKY AFFIRMATIONS

When you're feeling down, repeat these menacing mantras
to get your blood pumping again.

IT'S SCARY HOW SMART I AM.

MY POWERS GROW
STRONGER EVERY DAY.

I AM KILLING IT.

DON'T POISON MY THOUGHTS...
I AM AMAZING AND I AM STRONG.

I WILL NOT BE A LAZYBONES.

I WILL NOT BE UNRAVELED.

I AM NOT AFRAID.
I LOVE FEAR TOO MUCH.

KEEP CALM AND SCARY ON.

I AM DESERVING OF TREATS
–NO TRICKS AND ALL TREATS.

I AM BEWITCHING. I AM MAGIC.

NOTHING CAN KILL MY VIBE.

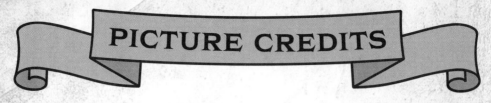

PICTURE CREDITS

REFERENCES

16 "Woe is the Loneliest Number", *Wednesday*, created by Alfred Gough and Miles Millar, season 1, episode 2, November 23, 2022, Netflix, https://www. netflix.com/title/81231974; 29 Dickinson, E (2005) *The Poems of Emily Dickinson* Variorum Edition, (Cambridge, Mass., and London); 34 Lovecraft, H P (2014) *The Complete Fiction of H P Lovecraft*, Race Point Publishing; 48 "Woe is the Loneliest Number", *Wednesday*, created by Alfred Gough and Miles Millar, season 1, episode 2, November 23, 2022, Netflix, https://www.netflix. com/title/81231974; 61 Shelley, M (1992), *Frankenstein* (Wordsworth Classics); 72 Siouxsie Sioux (2005), as quoted in "Her dark materials" by Michael Bracewell in *The Guardian*; 80 "Wednesday's Child Is Full of Woe", *Wednesday*, created by Alfred Gough and Miles Millar, season 1, episode 1, November 23, 2022, Netflix, https://www.netflix.com/title/81231974; 84 Poe, E A (2021), *Edgar Allan Poe: The Ultimate Collection*; 92 Radcliffe, A (2008) *The Mysteries of Udolpho*, Oxford World's Classics